A SILENT TEAR

Edited by

Natalie Nightingale

First published in Great Britain in 2001 by
POETRY NOW
Remus House,
Coltsfoot Drive,
Peterborough, PE2 9JX
Telephone (01733) 898101
Fax (01733) 313524

HB ISBN 0 75432 696 9
SB ISBN 0 75432 697 7

FOREWORD

Although we are a nation of poets we are accused of not reading poetry, or buying poetry books. After many years of listening to the incessant gripes of poetry publishers, I can only assume that the books they publish, in general, are books that most people do not want to read.

Poetry should not be obscure, introverted, and as cryptic as a crossword puzzle: it is the poet's duty to reach out and embrace the world.

The world owes the poet nothing and we should not be expected to dig and delve into a rambling discourse searching for some inner meaning.

The reason we write poetry (and almost all of us do) is because we want to communicate: an ideal; an idea; or a specific feeling. Poetry is as essential in communication, as a letter; a radio; a telephone, and the main criterion for selecting the poems in this anthology is very simple: they communicate.

CONTENTS

COLD, COLD MY LOVER'S BED

Cold is the bed wherein my lover lies,
Dark above, the exultant waiting skies,
Oh cull his soul from this his mortal flesh,
I drench his grave with my tears afresh.

Just one day has he been in his nest,
With hands reposed upon his silent breast,
Whilst I have kept my vigil for a year,
Or so it seems to my poor heart sincere.

Oh I would take his place within the tomb,
So he could lie once more within the womb,
And burst to life, and set this world aflame,
I'd sell my soul if he could live again.

The die is cast. I cannot draw aside
The veil of death that shrouds his empty eyes,
Could I but kiss his mouldering lips once more,
I feel my passion could his form restore.

Oh list, oh list, I think I hear him stir,
Beneath the loamy soil, he speaks! - To Her!
Once more the hatred beats within my heart,
I wish 'twas she my knife had torn apart.

But 'twas my dearest love that I had slain,
His love for me had withered, oh the pain!
I still can feel the knife twist in his chest,
As to his bloody mouth my lips I pressed.

So I am left here weeping with my shame,
Whilst she walks free, the one who was to blame,
He beckons me. The blade glints through the gloom,
If I cannot share his life, I'll share his tomb!

Susan Edwards

THE CHEATING KID

You think you're fooling me - shame 'cos I was 100% true
You've had numerous warnings now I'm leaving you
I'm going out the door and never coming back
Don't come running after me, I've had all I can hack.

You had me fooled so you thought, or at least it was said
Shame my heart took a bypass and I thought with my head
Tongues have started wagging I've been seen on the town
My happy-go-lucky style has gone, my smile has turned into a frown.

I sat down deep in thought and really thought things through
An answer soon came to me - 'do unto others as they do to you'
You won't break my heart again, you won't get half a chance
If you pass me in the street you won't get a second glance.

My heart is shattered into a million pieces
I'm trying to get over you - the pain it never ceases
I'm looking strong on the outside - there's nowhere to hide
But like water on a sandcastle, I'm crumbling inside.

Stay with my own kind that's what I'll do
No women involved in my life to make me feel blue
I'll stay with my own kind, my heart fully intact
I'm coming to terms with it all, I'm never coming back.

Leigh Smart

LOST

Left to my silence
I need your kiss,
your lips to prise mine open
breathe them into speech.

Sitting, one to a sofa,
leaning on its arm,
I want your grip
firm against my shoulder
confirming warmth,
banishing the cold space beside me.

Alone in bed
I mourn your body,
will some special power
to bring you close -
fold me in.

I see us
where now I see the void:
empty of you.

Sue Britchford

ROSES IN THE SNOW

Love and laughter in our home
Feelings so tender flowing through the phone
Music our companion when we were apart
Binding us together, silver streamers
Around our hearts
The roses in December, you gave them every year
But the ones I will remember my whole life through
Are those that seemed to grow through the snow
That grey and terrible day I said goodbye to you
The pain will never go away
Though there will be golden days
For my heart and mind will always remember
Your touch and the love in your eyes
The way you made everyone smile
But inside your heart was surely breaking
Knowing that you would soon be gone
You left behind a wealth of understanding
And gave me strength to carry on
For the little time we had was filled with happy hours
Building precious memories to recall
When dark clouds do appear
So every year I take roses to the place where you now lay
And thank God I knew you
If only for a while.

M P Holmes

LET DOWN

Leave him come and live with me
You said it every day
We're meant to be together
In every kind of way.

You fill my life, I love you
You often said to me
So leave your man immediately
And come and live with me.

But you have got a wife I said
And you will never leave
She needs your presence in the home
And you know you are weak.

Oh no, I can do it
You often said to me
So leave your man immediately
And come and live with me.

And after many episodes
Of begging me to go
I left my man to be with you
But you just couldn't go.

And when I said to you, what now?
You've left me in a mess
You knew I couldn't do you said
What more could I expect.

Denise Tidswell

HEROES

This man,
Iago or Heathcliff
invites me to go on a
pilgrimage to seek my
soul's mate.

I look
Hero or villain
at the dry clutter of
a devalued life and
question.

The rocks
Immutable gave
life to meaning when young
in maturity weigh less
than air.

I ask
my friends to spare me
deception - you can only
be unhappy this is
no worse.

Answer.
To know that to seek
dispels inertia and the
dream that the sought may be
in time.

Accept.
Challenge or failure
travel towards the hope
of consummated late
desire.

Losers?
Iago or Heathcliff
The expression of loves'
passion is never
abstract.

L A Churchill

I WANT OF US

I want you to phone, and say you're sorry.
For, what you did to me.
To really see . . . that you did wrong . . . your fault entirely.
I want you to apologise.
And, ask if you can write . . .
To me, as a friend . . .
Saying we will no longer fight.
The tensions between us, have no rhyme or reason.
You snap at me . . . I snap at you . . . like the silly season.
This is of no use at all . . . and uses up our energy.
When . . . the same amount of effort could make us friends.

Though the differences between us, are hard to overcome.
Just think how nice it would be.
If this war we won . . . together.

A friendship . . . until the end of time.
Would be our reward.
Instead . . . of both of us . . . falling on our swords.
We are not, Geisha or Samurai, from another time.
But we had something, not of now . . .
Maybe feelings from previous climes.
There are stranger things . . . they say.
Than are dreamt in our philosophy.

Sheila Mack

THE TEARDROP TREE

Will you walk with me to the Teardrop tree
That grows at the rainbow's end?
Will you spare one thought for my misery
Or shed a tear where my heart strings bend?

See the teardrop drip from the Teardrop tree;
Feel the pain as they fill my eyes;
Come, Sweet Girl, share my reverie,
For life gets sweeter before it dies.

Walk softly away from the Teardrop tree
That grows at the rainbow's end;
For now you know of my misery
As you feel your heart strings bend.

Jeevar

AND SHALL I LOVE THEE LESS?

And shall I love thee less because you're gone
To that far home beyond the skies,
To live hopefully in peace and harmony
Whilst my heart bleeds and dies?

And shall I love thee less because I cannot see you?
You fill my mind and heart though thou art out of sight,
All moments of the now dreary days
And endless, sleepless nights.

And shall I love thee less because you're physically gone?
The memories of you and I together will forever linger on,
My heart is yours lovingly now as the first day we met,
Pray, Allah keep you safe, until I to you can get.

Vivian Khan

LILITH PASSING BY

Her face lit up as though
for a kiss
But we passed like strangers
that night in the street,
My Lilith that was
before Eve.

Why did we meet before
why did we love before
why meet again now?
Oh joy of an old love
waking!

But gone again now
gone down the street,
My Lilith that was
before Eve.

Michael Rowson

LOVE IS

Love is a journey
Buzzard's drifting lift,
Hill fort spirals.

The mother's touch
A father's grasp
The inner child.

Orion's studded belt
Moon stepped times
Helicon scented breezes.

White water rivers,
Smooth tongue lilt
Slatted thunder bursts.

Water curtain falls
Shoulders bearing river
Head iced cold.

Sand martins dancing,
Egress feathered flight,
Marram coastal dunes.

Sun longed shores
Aegean blue spectrum
Sand baked toes.

Heat trapped hair,
Soil black nails,
Toiled earth rest.

Open night sky,
Lake burnt faces
Ember grey laughter.

Red ochre dust,
Blazed Southern Cross,
Life's tangent cycles.

John Greeves

HEART TO HEART

Right now I feel so all alone and lost,
The words I always listen for are no longer heard.
I did not say goodbye, I did not see you leave,
Somehow I am expected to hide away my emotions.
My heart cries out for you to be close,
I wait so long for you to come and wipe my tears away.
I scream out your name over and over again,
Sounding so desperate I fall to the ground.
The long summer nights seem a waste now you're gone,
Those walks we both enjoyed are lonely on my own,
At night in bed I cry with my hands to my face,
Finally I fall asleep and awake with red swollen eyes.
I feel I have lost a part of my world, that is you,
I am unable to face life alone without you here.
I long to know if I will ever see you again,
Wishing so much I could feel your lips against mine.
I miss you so much I am torn apart inside,
My love for you will grow stronger even though you're absent,
Nothing in this whole world ever seems fair,
Is it so bad for two people in love to want to be happy?

Zoe Fitzjohn

A SONG OF LOVE

O sweet oblivion, render me immune
To memories of the one I loved and lost,
By my ill-fated stars perversely crossed,
Bedazzled by a mediaeval tune.

He sang of courtly love in days of old,
Of damsels rescued from a donjon tower
By errant knights from Camelot - the flower
Of Arthur's realm, adventurous and bold.

His tuneful ballad touched a cord in me -
A minstrel song of courtship and romance,
With words by troubadours from Annecy,
And measured rhythms of a stately dance.
But when he tired of the melody,
He walked away without a backward glance.

Celia G Thomas

THE SECRET LOVERS

Upon a tree, is carved,
hard into its missing bark;
the sad, tragic tale of two lovers, who gave to each,
their lives, their hearts.

'Destiny, my destiny,' said he, 'has been not misguided,
for you, my Venus, my Fallen Star, had glided,
one last time into my awaiting arms,
I am your prisoner, captivated, forever, by your loving charms.'

'Alas,' she replied, through weepy eyes, 'I ache for you,
but also knew the course-path-love that's true,
twists and turns and ne'er runs smooth -
To have that of which I can never have, to cherish, to love,
for all time, can e'er my love, be reproved.'

'Aye,' he sighed, their hands entwined.
'You are married, and I, betrothed,
But as I gaze into eyes that blaze, a passion burns,
profound, within my soul.
So speaks truth of eternal, forbidden love that must
stay the test and ne'er grow; to grace face with stains of tears,
tidings tales of woe.

So now,' quivered he, lips kissing gently, her salt falling tears.
'My most precious love, tis time to part lest we,
for what we are, be discovered, shamed before all by
some poor, blubbering fool who speaks truth of which
we cannot hide, or deny, and thus will surely say:'
'This day their hearts entwined, for I found these
two obscure from truth!
Look! The Secret Lovers!

And as she faded into that solemn, jaded night,
I wrote verse upon this bark, before I took my life.
For promise, did she, faithfully, to meet me here,
by this ere, old oak tree, and now, I too must go,
for my love, my precious love, awaits, most patiently.'

And look! Behold! Two spirits merge, hand in hand they span the
course, as one celestial, heavenly glow -
So ends the tale of the Secret Lovers' tragedy, for now, all's been told.

Glenwyn Peter Evans

THAT MAN OF MINE

Today, I am not at all well.
In fact I feel a total hell.
What I'm doing, or where going,
I wish, really, I were knowing.

It is all a problem with him.
It's he who's making my life grim.
So lost am I without him there,
My life, alone, I cannot bear.

It's not too much what he has done
That has so upset all my fun.
He won't give me even a glance,
Yet sends me into such a trance.

P'rhaps tomorrow will be better,
But he has me in true fetter.
I deeply love him oh, so much
And it's awful when not in touch.

I can't encourage him much more,
For he knows it's him I adore.
Where, on earth, do I go from here?
I'm going to lose him, I fear.

Is there a doctor within reach
Or a fairy I can beseech?
And where is my own mother dear?
I'm so sick and need someone here.

What medicine is there for the heart,
When from your love you are apart?
They say Father Time is the best,
But with him I'm quite unimpressed!

Susan Audrey

YOU

I look in the mirror,
I see you.
You drop a kiss upon my head,
As you always do.
I lift a brush and stroke my hair,
You pretend to do the same.
It's just a little game you like to play.
You pick up a lipstick
And write my name
And I love you
And your name too.
Then you walk to and fro
And I shout, 'Don't go! Don't go!'
And you are there beside me.
I am deep in thought for a minute,
I look in the mirror once again.
There is nothing in it.
It's just a little game I like to play,
Hoping you will come back to me.
Am I telling myself lies?
Tears are in my eyes.
I see them in my reflection,
You are there to wipe away my tears
Or perhaps it was a vision.
I feel such a fool;
Sitting on my stool,
Gazing in the mirror,
My dear, my dear,
Has the magic gone forever?

Beth Anderson

BEWITCHED

She came to me in glorious splendour,
Winged chariots on clouds of fire,
She came to me in deep December,
Inflamed my heart with such desire.

With raven hair as black as midnight,
Eyes burning like the brightest coals,
Bedecked in jewels of sparkling starlight,
She pierced the centre of my soul.

I was blinded by her brightness,
Bewitched by her beguiling charm,
Bedazzled by her fleeting lightness,
Believed that she could do no harm.

I loved her, as I'd loved no other,
'Neath holly boughs and mistletoe,
Entwined in ivy, loved and lover,
The new year came, where did she go?

I gaze into the dying embers,
Alone and empty, nothing's left,
A hollow shell, try to remember,
My heart, my soul, broken, bereft.

They say it's my imagination,
That I'm insane, gone off my head,
But I remember, with elation,
The fevered passions of our bed.

The embers flare and flame, I see her,
Calling me to join her there,
My heart tells me that it will be her,
I reach out, touch her raven hair.

Jim Sargant

SHE TOOK YOU FROM ME

I loved you more than life itself,
You were the reason I woke every morning,
To see you smile - to feel your warm breath against my cheek.
Just hearing you utter a single word could make my heart skip a beat.

When we were together, nothing else mattered,
Embraced within your powerful arms - I knew I was safe.
I thought that nobody would ever come between us,
Until *she* came along.

She changed it all,
Everything we had both worked so hard to preserve shattered
before my eyes,
As if it were a delicate glass incautiously hurled at a brick wall.
Why did you do this to me?

It felt like part of me was missing - my heart,
I can't believe you were so easily led astray.
I thought you loved me,
I guess I was wrong.

I can't bear to see you with her,
Laughing, kissing, hugging - we used to be like that!
There's only one solution now,
If I can't have you, nobody else can . . .

O A Daley

JUST A FEELING

Just a feeling I had with you
Like nobody else would ever do
You didn't feel the same
You left me with just a feeling to blame
Just a feeling in my heart
That you could bring me together or tear me apart
Even now not a day goes by
A feeling like this won't ever die
Just a feeling that I need you more
I'd never felt like that before
I cried and prayed, day and night
The feeling remained but you were out of sight

Amanda Steel

IF
(To my wife, Joyce)

If I could kindle the flame in your heart
To bring purpose to your life
Never more for us to part
Could you be my wife?

If I could honour and protect you my love
With tender loving care - undefiled
If I could do those things above
Could you bear my child?

If I could with all sincerity provide
Companionship my dear
And explain this feeling deep inside
Could you say yes - to dispel my fear?

Billy Rose

LOVING YOU

These were nature's windows,
  Touching Heaven and Earth,
Constable filling the corners,
  Renoir in my heart
You were my September window,
  Tossing berries in my lap,
Sewing oats into my winter of discontent.

I was wiser,
  So I thought,
Bright pink 'Beardsley' prints,
  Outrageous behaviour,
Painted eyes that winked
  Picasso nudged my emotions,
In every shade of blue,
  When I'd lost the time
To keep on loving you.

My window now,
  Sees only shades of grey,
I cannot see or touch you,
  And the moon
Won't light the sky . . .

Margarette Phillips

ALONE

What is the point of life now you have gone?
I've simply lost the will to carry on.
Time was, when each new day was filled with fun.
The morning sky, all bright with promised sun.
My eyes are blinded now to all these things.
The wonder of it all has taken wings.
How could a love like ours just simply die,
Was everything you ever said a lie?

You never did explain, just left a note,
I read it now, while tears ache in my throat.
'I'm sorry if I've caused you any pain,
Perhaps one day, sometime, we'll meet again'
Such casual, empty words they seem to be,
While all my world comes crashing down, for me.

My heart is like a desert, dead and dry,
My soul so numb, I don't know how to cry.
They say that time will heal a broken heart,
But time for me has ceased, now we're apart.

Amelia Wilson

LOVE AND LUST

Submit my spirit in lust's traitor fashion
To make desire's proud emperor my liege
And like a mercenary, fight for gain,
Leaving honour to satisfy my passion?
How can you ask my heart to poorly ration
Among those sirens its dearest pain?
Oh you've never borne the terrible siege;
Your soul's never trembled at the dread name's sounding.
It falls on me, that shadow in all places,
In fury, ardour, terror. You go bounding.
After the dust a phantom's mad paces
Raise like a mirage of love's last reality.
Your shallow laughing friendship's a dark stain
Of beauty slain by sleek and light banality.

Uvedale Tristram

KEEPING HER IN MEMORY

A blue space in the clouds
Where my heaven peeps through . . .

A soft voice in the night
When I'm dreaming of you . . .

A mere sifting of sand
Are the thoughts in my mind . . .

A short passing of time
Since you left me behind . . .

But the time has seemed long
And weighs heavy at heart;
Its keeping's a burden,
Each sweet memory's a part
Of my staying alive,
Of me breathing life's air,
For of you there's our child
Who is needing my care . . .

Our child will continue
Along life's winding lane,
So I'll guide her with love
Till I meet you again . . .

Still true to your memory -
In her eyes *you* will shine -
Our thoughts will be of you
Till the end of our time . . .

Mary Pauline Winter

LOVE BLUES

When you're away, the breath of life
which makes the hell worthwhile
goes with you;

suffocated thus -
listless, zest deprived -
I miss the wand tip touch
of kindling spark which only you
dispense to give my life a purpose;

and in my eye, thus filtered dark,
other people seem as separate
rank-based zombie tribes
playing out their predetermined
automated mah-jong lives -

illusions, once accepted,
shatter to reveal their cardboard contents'
shabby worth;
cloth paint-daubed scenes of everyday
dry and rot away
revealing the frailty of the landscape
structure they had gaily hid

soul-less, thus, the scene reverts -
dust to dust, ecclesiasticus -
because you, my sun and moon and stars in one
have gone and left me,
even for day.

Edward Fursdon

A LIFETIME APART

When you glimpse the stars at night,
Think of me.
When you feel the warm summer sun,
Think of me.

In a child's laugh,
Think of us;
In the rhythm of the waves,
Think of us.

In the scent of a rose,
In the caress of a breeze,
In the beat of the music,
Think of us.

I will be there.

Helen Smith

SELDOM AND OFTENTIMES:
A TALE OF WOE AND WONDER

Oftentimes it is but joy we can delay,
For pain will always catch us up one day,
Or, in failing as captor, to punisher turns,
Now to make of us fools ever spurned.

Seldom is it love that forfeits tears,
A melody of woe is sung upon deaf ears,
But hearing or not cannot make it stop,
For the notes carry on a-gallop.

Time again it is death which us parts,
The tear from the eye as blood from the heart,
Up in the clouds as in miseries afar,
Heavenly reach into innocence marred.

Helen Marshall

MY BEAUTIFUL GIRL

Where did she go? That beautiful girl,
The one that I loved so much,
She was my angel, my princess, my pearl,
I craved her kiss and her touch.

With beauty and grace and dressed so fine,
Her smile was so appealing,
Her on my arm, I'm proud she is mine,
How I really loved that feeling.

The words of love she spoke to me,
I believed them, with all I was worth,
Because with her, I wanted to be,
I'd have gone to the ends of the earth.

We went through lots of good times and bad,
With loads of trouble and strife,
But I remember the good times we had,
For her I'd have laid down my life.

She went away and left me alone,
She said she just couldn't stay,
I felt torn, was cut to the bone,
How hurt I was on that day.

So where did she go? The love that I had,
She disappeared so it would seem,
But I mustn't, I cannot, I shouldn't feel bad,
Perhaps she was only a dream.

Stephen Miller

FOR RICH, I LOVE YOU BECAUSE!

For Rich, I love you because . . .
though I am a writer and even a poet,
writing how I feel about you is still very hard to do.
To start with, I love you because you are you!

I love you because you make me feel intensely,
You give me such a range of emotions, how little you know.
I love you because you share your soul.
You let me see how beautiful you are to me!

To write the truth and depth of feeling
without flattery is hard.
I love you because of your creativity,
your Pisces-Scorpion way.

I can see God in you, you share that with me.
You are the most empathetic, sympathetic, compassionate,
caring, forgiving person I know.
You care so much about others especially the less fortunate,
and you don't just sit around talking about how you can help,
you go out and do something about it.

I love you because you are my gatekeeper
(you and I know why and what that is).
I can fall asleep knowing you watch over me.
I speak of the spiritual things there.

So as for the physical, you are very cute for sure.
This you may or may not know,
every one of us has a secret heart's desire
(you know mine includes publication and you help me to achieve that)
my real secret heart's desire is you!

But that's not fair, I have to let you go!
You have to choose love for yourself.
I wish you well and all the happiness love brings.
I am glad to be a part of it.

I love you because after all this time,
you still get under my skin.
I love you because you are my special and best friend always.
Love Cheryl.

Cheryl Carlyle

TELL ME HOW

Can you tell me how my love,
How I can forget you.
Can you show me how love,
How I can reject you.
Can you tell me how,
To repair my broken heart.
Show me if you can love,
How to make a brand new start.

I need some help from someone to redirect my life,
My mind is in a turmoil,
My thoughts are running rife.
If anyone should ask me just what should I do,
I will have to answer nothing!
For life is nothing without you.

Molly Ann Kean

WHERE THE EAGLE FLIES

I wept for you my dearest
As we shared your parting sigh
Now I look for you where the eagle flies
You are the spirit in his eyes
And as he reaches the beckoning clouds
In his soaring, spiral flight
My being no longer feels the pain
In the bright ethereal light
And as you leave these earthly ties
On your final journey home
His wings caress the healing rain
And his body absorbs the sun
Sweeping away my pain
I look for you in his effortless flight
His feathery head upturned
For here is where your spirit flies
Upward towards the light
And if I feel a drop of rain
Brush my waxen cheek
I smile the smile of contentment my love
For he has brushed away my pain
As the powerful wings of the eagle
Carry you back home
And when the fields are a sea of gold
With the flowers reaching for the sun
I will listen for the cry of the eagle
His quest is almost done
For as long as the wind carries the eagle's wings
He is your spirit that forever flies.

Mel Bartliff

MY LOVE, SWEET VISION
(After Elizabeth Barrett Browning)

My love, sweet vision
Of a beauty thought.
When first our eyes did seek
A shelter there.
A promise, chaste, a golden touch,
So soft, for love's sake.
Where upon the brow
I plant a lover's oath,
A kiss, and thus my spirit guides.
For my hope forward flows
Until we can, our fingers touch as one,
And walk together
On the shore, our life begun.
For so, my love, my whisper
Held forever in your heart,
Upon a rock we build
A life of trust
And soon our time together
Be forever.

Melanie Anne Camp

AND SOMETIMES LOVE JUST SLIPS AWAY

I watched a woman die one quiet night:
I held her in my arms as life just ebbed away.
I kissed her final breath to say goodbye:
My best friend of half my life simply left that day.

And sometimes love just slips away,
Like dry sand runs through open fingers.

It was bad enough to tell her mother,
Then the children woke to find an empty chair.
A year or more of suffering was concluded,
But how do you speak into the heartbroken stare?

And sometimes love just slips away,
Like dry sand runs through open fingers.

You felt your marriage die one quiet night:
His words cut through sixteen years and pierced your heart.
You'd seen the writing on the wall so long before,
But for other's sake you tried to make another start.

And sometimes love just slips away,
Like dry sand runs through open fingers.

It was bad enough to feel rejected,
Then your children had to hear the awful news.
And time has dealt some other painful blows,
Simply through the freedom they have in life to choose.

And sometimes love just slips away,
Like dry sand runs through open fingers.

But God remains to do the clearing up.

Bob White

FOND FAREWELL

A tearful reunion but a fond farewell
Is what we've had today
May all your hopes be realised
In every possible way

It was bliss when we were together
But we knew it was not meant to be
We gradually drifted apart
At least now you can be free

I hope you learn to love again
In all you try to do
While I wait here in solitude
With only thoughts of you

Philip O'Leary

JACOB'S WEDDING

Jacob fell in love with Rachel
he asked her father for her hand
this was agreed provided Jacob
worked seven years on his land.

So Jacob worked for seven years
keeping to the agreement
this time the wedding feast was
planned and invitations sent.

During the wedding ceremony
the groom stood transfixed
as his bride lifted her veil
Jacob knew that he'd been tricked.

For it was not his bride
Rachel, that he had just wed
but her elder sister Leah
that he'd just married instead.

Jacob tried speaking to his
father-in-law at the reception
to let him know of his
displeasure at this deception.

Jacob felt unjustly treated
but the custom, Laban said
his youngest daughter couldn't marry
until his eldest girl was wed.

Laban then told Jacob that
to have his daughter Rachel
by working seven more years
he could marry her as well.

Moon Stone

DAYDREAMS

I keep watching for your face
As each day passes
I scan the crowds looking for your smile
But you don't come and the pain won't leave
My solitude is endless
How far away those days of love
The memory never passes
And the fashions they may come and go
My daydreams they don't change
Just the people and the scenery
I don't suppose she spares a thought for me
After all the hurts I caused
But if I live another live
It will still be for her that I search

Les Allen

LOVE IN A MODERN VAIN

Once, there was a man
(Of course it *had* to be a man),
Who adored himself so much
He was his own biggest fan.
On moonlit nights he'd sigh
And wonder why his love was thus,
When seeing his reflection
It was never him but 'us'.
Being infatuated with his image
Actuated him to fill
His lonesome home with mirrors,
A narcissistic idyll.
Reflecting on the way he looked,
Dissecting all the reasons why
One man should be so lovely.
He could never say goodbye
To the one that he adored
So he hoarded himself away,
Locked inside his mansion
Self-romancing night and day.
Years passed, and nothing lasts,
His hair turned white and fell;
The once-slight figure ran to fat
And in his private Hell,
Reminded by the mirrors everywhere
He smashed every one.
Broken glass came raining down
Till most of him was gone;
And so to be sure the last would depart
He thrust a shard into his shattered heart.

Jonathan Goodwin

SHADOWS OF MEMORIES

Whispers in a gentle breeze
Echo memories
Like rustle of leaves
Memories, so long ago
Plans and promises
All went astray
Wonder where you are today
Happiness was ours
We thought forever
But fate took a hand
And changed our plans
If by chance
We met again
Could our happiness
Be as before
Fate step'd in and closed the door?
Could we open the door
And start again?
It is so hard to tell
But oh! for a wishing well.

Margaret Parnell

UNTIL WE MEET, WITH HIM . . .

'Star-crossed love' . . . strange words t'me:
   A star, is what our Lord has made;
Crossed? Well, what can that mean, that be?
   A path, that's crossed? A heart that's crossed?
I shall, now, try to see . . .

A 'star' is what they name, with fame,
   The ones that hit the headline . . .
The ones that play this sad, world's game
   And boast of doin' fine:
Do they glibly drink, ignore the 'lame'?

Crossed? . . . A path? I hope, that I
   N'er cross a path, to make an enemy!
Crossed: The heavens, where God's Cross
   Is shining, both for you and me,
And showing us: His pain, His loss,

That we, who believe, can be forgiven
   Our sins from start to end;
And offered His place in Heaven -
   To learn t'obey Him . . . be His friend,
With His true love, as our leaven . . .

Love: Well! That's a key word, isn't it?
   The meaning of all that He's done
By offering His Life: Thru His death, make us fit
   To dwell with the One, begotten Son -
Overcoming the world, and - the git!

By git, I mean God's enemy . . .
   And love must always (it seems) suffer
In the fight, to set love free,
   With Jesu's Blood as our buffer
Until, we meet with Him, in His eternity . . .

Anon

QUEER

Two star-crossed lovers,
With twinkles in their eyes,
Forced to live their lives,
Behind a shadow of lies.

Pretending to love their girls,
As much as the good Lord,
What they do is right,
But yet it feels like fraud.

Yet there's something else,
That's buried deep inside,
The chance to reveal which,
Has long since lived and died.

So they go on being friends,
And denying their burning lust,
Being careful not to make a slip,
And betray their darling's trust.

So they sit at the bar,
Laughing and supping beer,
If they were to show their love,
They'd only be branded as queer.

Kimberly Jamie

FIRST LOVE DIES

Though time has slowly passed
My love for you will always last
Time changes many things
And our song I'll always sing

But time will also change my life
Perhaps I'll be another's wife
But though I may be with another
You were always my first love

My love and memories will never die
Watch out for me from the sky
You and I will never part
Though another may take my heart

I will smile and hold his hand
And then I know I understand
That life has given me a chance
And again I'll love and dance

Irene Pizey

THE SONNET

My heart near drops and breaks when you but move
And something there inside me slowly dies
I'm tortured by the love I can't remove
I see the haunting passion in your eyes.
And them the stars themselves do envy most!
I'm short of breath just dreaming of your kiss
'I have a love that's true!' I hear them boast
And I would too if you should feel like this.
I'm half a person, curse my weary mind
My heart is full of you and turning weak
And curse as well this thought: 'O! Love is blind'.
I never met your eyes or heard you speak
O, unrequited love, I curse your name.
My love for him shall always stay the same.

Holly Dymock (13)

FORBIDDEN LOVE

The bare branches sway:
Natural couched lances
Pointing at my heart,
Thundering down the lists
Of my forbidden love
To wreak their vengeance
For my unnatural crime
Against the cruel Lord
Who is owed my sweeting's
Obedience by right.
Meekly must I
Bare my breast to
The avenging trees;
Bow my head;
Avert my eyes; accept
The bitter pain of
Their terminal bite
As fitting mortification
And go to my death
Without the annealing
Comfort of God's forgiveness:
Doomed to the eternal flames
By the limbs that
Feed our mortal fires.
I have no right to mercy.

Ted Harriott

WITHOUT

Excluded from your arm
Unwanted in your thoughts
Two dreamers pulled apart
And I am left without.

Missing how you miss me
When hands are touching face
Blind to how it happened
Seen to be ignored.

If keeping is to steal
I take and you will stay
Unaided though I am
Still to be without.

Lee Severns

NOT TO BE

I saw the look upon your face
As I looked in through the door
I knew exactly what you meant
'Twill live with me for evermore
Our two hearts were joined as one
No words needed, that look could speak
I felt my life entwined in you
In my heart it's you I keep
I've travelled far, I've travelled wide
Down the years that look doth stay
But you were married to someone else
And now my love you're far away

George Camp

THE END

Have you ever had the feeling that you just don't want to live?
Have you ever had them take from you all you have to give?
Have you ever felt as if the world is always blaming you?
Have you ever felt you've done it all with nothing more to do?
Have you ever felt rejected, tired and confused?
Have you ever felt that both your mind and body have been used?
Have you ever felt the sunshine in your life has turned to rain?
Have you ever felt that all the tears you've cried have been in vain?
Have you ever felt that all your love has slowly turned to hate?
Have you ever felt it's time to go, no longer can you wait?
Have you ever felt that now your broken heart will never mend,
And all that's left for you to do is bring life to an end?

S Brown

CHAMELEON

Long time waiting, under the lime,
the road ahead bordered by scent,
meandering through small paths, crystalline
days where the red sky swells the heart.

Switch to another time:
black beetles on a wallflowered dawn
where shadows walk on their own
and stars are swaddled in milky spawn.

And the chameleon places her tongue
on ancient landscapes ripped and torn
where the songthrush leaves her song unsung,
her passion cruelly thwarted.

Kick the earth, shroud the sun.
Forked trees in an island storm.
A picture develops, the colours run
blazing past the eagle's nest;

her burnished eggs of solid gold
lay brazen, guardless in their Everest.
The howl is out, the shadow cold,
A rage upon a sapling breast.

A memory pulsing a purple vein,
the atavistic threads of silk
weave their fertile counterpane
on bleak, decaying, stark terrain.

And the chameleon weeps her childhood's pain.

Wendy Poole

LEVELS OF LOVE

The world is full of love
First acquaintances are new
With a ray of spiritual light
Warmth and friendship grew

Many people all around
Then there was just us two
Lots of things to be achieved
We stuck together like glue

Homeward bound along the road
Never knowing where to park
Turning right on stony ground
Two feet from your matriarch

Up and around the steps we climb
Ever higher to the light
Beholding letters drawn alike
Burning candles in the night

Journey far across the levels
All you want is for a song
Meeting folk in distant parts
Getting lost be not for long

Holding tight to make you well
Loving friendship does abound
Feasting prawns from foreign parts
Now we know our friendship's sound

Steve Lattimore

TURN AROUND

she never loved me, that I know
she came, she left, now there's no trace
of the love I knew, for in her face
was no fond look, no breathless waiting for my kiss
her heart was cold, we were no match
just a memory of sadness upon my heart

the grief - there it was, bitter and dark
the hate dissipated and joy was found
life now has meaning, treasures do abound
my love now is gleaming and hope is in store
life it is new, like a child's at birth
and the days they are dawning, the sun it does shine . . .

for my love it is burning for all mankind.

William C E Howe

HE WAS UNFORGETTABLE

My bosom mate died in his prime
I was devastated, left a wounded wife
We were forever one person
My heart was severely broken
No one has ever taken his place
He will always be my sacred lover
Devout love lasts forever

Alma Montgomery Frank

NIGHT PERFORMERS

Romeo loved Juliet loved with true silent voices
Their elegy was solemn sung
And artfully they lived and died
When words alone were failing
The proof was in their theme tune
The epitome in their names
As an angry star went rampaging
And blazed the tale of foolish loves
And lovers' fools
Loaded in the stars
Love-sickened
Tragedy is the disguise
Without face.

C A Thompson

HEATHCLIFF

Long ago, we ran free together, over the windswept moor
I thought we would run so forever, imagined our destiny sure
Blithely, we ran through the tempest, the storm raged in our blood
The passing of years has not tamed me, nor my passion subdued
Together, we were one spirit - one soul, together, we made
But sundered from you, I am nothing, not even a shade
Though wicked fate chose to part us, our souls are still one
                                        and the same
On the wind that blows from the churchyard I hear you
                            whisper my name
If Hera came down from Olympus and offered herself as my muse
And Aphrodite beguiled me, still, Cathy I'd choose
I hear your voice, in the stillness, hear your tread on the stair
I feel your shadow pass near me, sense your presence close by my chair
With cruel deceit, you prevent me from seeing you clear
Half angel, half devil, you torment me - so far off, so near
Stay, vengeful spirit, and haunt me - tear out my soul!
With your half-seen presence, you taunt me, from your clay-bed,
                                    so cold
Soon, we will lie there together, close, side by side
There I'll rest, in my heaven, forever with my ghostly bride
Neither distance nor time can efface you from my bitter-wrung heart
As our dust mingles, so I'll embrace you; death shall not us part
A melancholy night bird is crying; the long day is done
Come to me, my dear love, I am dying - but you do not come

Leyna Brinkmeyer

REFLECTIONS

Kneeling, I see my face reflected in the still waters of the pool,
The face I know so well.
A gentle breeze ripples the surface and my reflection is twisted,
distorted,
I do not recognise this face,
Yet I know it to be mine.
Do I appear to others in a different way?
Perhaps when I am angry or disturbed
They see an unfamiliar face,
Not now those lineaments to which they are accustomed,
Expression worn to hide the grief of loss.

The surface of the pool is still and calm once more,
And as I gaze down into the depths,
Suddenly another face appears,
Another face beside my own.
It is a face I know and love,
We are together in the pool,
United once again.
Joyfully, I reach out to hold that face so dear.
My fingers touch the water.
Its surface is disturbed, no longer clear.
In anguish I withdraw my hands -
Too late - for you are gone.
My face alone remains.

What does this face reveal?
Loneliness, longing, desolation.
For one brief moment, my beloved,
We were as one again.
Now, as once before in death,
We are parted,
And I remain alone
To wear the mask that hides the pain.

Roma Davies

FUTURE

I have a date with you
between Russia and China
in Trans-Siberian train
in the vast wilderness
of outer Mongolia and Tibet

where we are going
Japan and Cambodia

- but the small space
in our heads carries
the burdens of the past
we cannot escape from
and scatter to the winds
of Siberian planes
but to live through
separately in our own pain
yesterday and today.

Marja von Ronkko

YES I LOVE YOU

Yes I love you.
Haven't I said?
The words that keep repeating in my head.
You know that I love you.
I've told you before
Less than a couple of days ago.

Yes I love you.
Don't be a fool.
I can't keep on being your emotional tool.
Believe that I love you.
I can't do more
I've told you and showed you my love is pure.

Yes. I love you.
You're making me mad.
Your insecurities are turning bad
The way that I love you
Can't you see?
This isn't the way that love should be.

I really did love you
But that love has died.
It was choked to death by your jealous side.
You know that I loved you.
But that love has gone.
So now is the time for me to move on.

Nadine Dunn

FRIENDS

Desolate alone am I
Friends departed
Leave pictures in my mind
Of things past
Not forgotten
Memories of loving times
Of hands entwined
Sunny days of
Sea, sand and laughter
Now silence hangs
Heavy in the air
An uncanny hush everywhere
And friends once here
Now gone
Leave their shadows.

Penny Kirby

LOVE

Love is such a tender trap,
We all pass this way, but then comes a scrap.
It is one of the greatest tests we must face,
Welcome it and you will grow in grace.

Don't think that because one remains single,
They don't know what it is like to jingle.
Fate was just not on their side,
And our generation had very few places in which to hide.

To those younger folk may I say as they grow in years,
Please have a little consideration for your peers.
It was to save you the indignities of life,
That the two great wars were so very rife.

Those of us who stayed alone,
Did so because it had to be done.
And that meant we did the lot,
Not two people sharing a plot.

A thing many will forever give thanks,
Is the way we learnt to combat most pranks.
It stood us all in very good stead.
At the same time teaching us to look ahead.

We know we missed a lot but we gained too,
And I for one send grateful thanks to you.
It is my belief that many blessings come with age,
And we are guided well even at this late stage.

Betty Green

Sonnet For An Autumn Evening

When I reflect on misspent youth and years,
And castigate my soul for sad neglect
Of all the lovely things that bring to tears
An honour which can never pay its debt,
I wonder if the love I might have known,
And all the joys so prodigally missed
Reproach me for my lethargy alone,
Or for the honeyed lips I might have kissed.
What other hearts regret the heart that spurned
Their siren rhapsodies, I cannot know,
But still I shed a tear for bridges burned
In reckless zeal some thirty years ago.
Now, as I muse on stirring deeds undone,
My heart bleeds for the girl I never won.

S H Smith

THE LADY WHO WALKS ALONE

Outside the canal side pub the stacked green plastic chairs
Cling to each other with damp kisses
In the autumn drizzle waiting
For a fickle sun to break cover,
But a brisk breeze tears through hope
And time despairs as the lady walks alone.
Passion mountain of fire hides deep inside and sleeps,
It can only escape through the passes
To the grassy plains below
Where soft green blades will not accept
Her fantasy dreaming,
While Heaven weeps for the lady who walks alone.
Piercing through the crimson cloud streams the white vapour trail
Of a jet liner marking the sky
With the sign of isolation
Dispersed into a white blush in space.
Her image holds to the mind
Leaving time to tell of the lady who walks alone.
Fragile dreams try to carry her awakening mind
Back to sleep but the morning breaks
The fantasies until she knows,
Today is her present reality
To be lived and endured,
For she can but be the lady who walks alone.
Beneath the copper beach trees waving leaves like hands
In the slight autumn breeze
She no longer stands
In the shadow they cast,
For free at last is the lady who walks alone.

Pat Isiorho

THE FINAL SCENE

We had agreed upon it
In a most civilised way.
In our prosaic times
Even the fiercest passion
Requires financial sustenance.
And so,
As you gathered your things,
I stood on the balcony
In the cruel sun,
While brown-limbed Italian boys
Frolicked below in the fantastic spray,
Their wild laughter
Mocking my emptiness.
Odours and sounds of an alien city
Assaulted my numbed senses.
All love's intensity
Wilted in mundaneness.
You came and kissed me,
Not in the ancient way -
But chastely, on the cheek,
And, to comfort your unease,
'I am content,' I said
And the door closed quietly behind you.

Jackie Lapidge

THE LEGEND OF TAMARA

('Traffic is flowing freely across the Tamar Bridge;
A ridge of high pressure is stationary over Cornwall . . .')

Long, long ago before the birth of man,
Earth spirits lived in caves beneath the land.
They dwelt in caverns far away from light;
Their graceful daughter was their true delight.
Beloved nymph Tamara loved to roam,
To climb into the dawn to play and dance
Where daisies kissed her feet and all was bright;
This paradise her parents held in fear,
For giants roamed, weird spirits would appear.

Yet still Tamara strayed to meet her friends
The giants of the moor, Tavy the bold,
Tawrage the brave; they both loved the fair maid.
They vowed their love for her could never fade.
But she must choose and thus her heart was torn;
Then, while she mused, her father came in rage;
He cursed her as a cruel, ungrateful jade.
He struck - the giants fell to earth to dream.
The nymph's hot tears became a gushing stream.

At last great Tavy woke; with broken heart
He sought his father who, to ease his pain
Changed him into a river, flowing clear
Which rushed o'er rocks and valleys to be near
His love. Tawrage, on waking, found a holy man
In haste, became a river, lost his way
Sorrowing ever in his lonely sphere.
While Tavy and Tamara mingled be,
Forever gliding t'wards th' eternal sea.

'Flood warnings have been issued for the Tamar,
the Tavy and the Taw . . .'

Anne James

DIDO AND AENEAS

Haughty queen of high renown,
lifeless, marble eyes cast down,
built a citadel of stone,
around her, where she lay alone.

Virgo and Cassiopeia wept,
drowned meteors while Carthage slept;
starstruck Dido, on her barge,
fastened on her new mirage.

With Maenad fury,
she burned like distant Troy,
and sleepless,
paced, for consummation
with her golden boy.

Jove bound them fast,
resounding claps and thrashing rain,
and, sheltering from his blast,
the two became,
as one.

Shimmering sweetly,
at last, he took his leave -
she stroked his chair, bereft,
for anything left of him,
she might retrieve.

Aeneas, turning,
faced the shore,
saw a burning cloud of fire,
and knew his guilt
had built
his tragic lady's funeral pyre.

Jennifer D Wootton

ROMEO'S JULY

Half-mast and limp flags are so sad
on a mid-July sunlit morning.

Grey shades tease and slowly stretch,
reflecting a night that is no more.

Death has kissed the swan upon the placid river
and left her without grace.

Her sky mate,
her soulmate love
knows not how to cry.

Yet, still he mourns.

A E S Gamage

MY SUFFERING

Oh Lord why have you taken
the one I treasured most
what was it that I did that was so wrong
she was young and she was beautiful
for you had made her so
but the time that you allowed us wasn't long

Our marriage in your holy house
your laws we vowed to keep
three children were to make our lives complete
love reigned within our household
and each day we praised your name
but then you came and took her in her sleep

And I forsook you, cursed and wept
for what you had done to me
my children and I could not understand
why take someone so full of love
and let evil people stay
I could not believe such cruelty you had planned

So now I roam this lonely world
with a cold, unfeeling heart
ever searching for some solace for my pain
and praying for the moment
when you will make me understand
and light the fire of love in me again.

Don Woods

TOGETHERNESS

The sun shone down to bless our companionship,
To dream the wasteland that was my life.
To make me realise that life's worth living,
And that I needn't live with trouble and strife.

We used to sit and talk for hours,
Contemplating what to do and who we were.
To understand what we're here for,
And that you needed me and I needed you.

But then the wind of change began,
And you started to change like the seasons.
I had then to accept with an aching heart,
That someone else had engulfed you.

Now walking through my life alone,
Each day another pain to bear.
And now I gaze out of my window,
And ache to find the happiness I once owned.

To again walk through the park hand in hand,
And feel the warmth that is to be truly needed.
Instead of the ache of a cooling heart,
That wonders if it will ever be loved.

So now I'll sit and gaze into oblivion,
Dreaming of the glory that was you and me.
And accept the fact that my life's without you,
And that's a pain I'll carry for eternity.

Mandi Paine

LIFE AFTER YOU

You came, you saw, the chase was on,
I foolishly let you conquer me;
The unknown was unable to warn me of what was to be.
Such charm and affection you poured over me,
When in your company, I loved and treasured every second,
Never dreaming you were not as you seemed to be.
Your charisma covered me as I hung onto your every word,
Basking in the delights only love can offer.
Gently you coaxed me, teased me and changed my life,
The beginning was magical and perfect. I walked on air;
But soon your caring mode altered, another persona took you over.
Your tenderness absented itself from time to time,
Having fingers in other pies, as you sampled new delights.
I was left hanging on for weeks sometimes, excuses made,
For the calls that never came, for your part-time love.
Reaching out for you, you ignored my needs,
I reeled on from day to day, trying to live without your nearness.
Only sinking deeper into my obsessive depressive state;
Hardly knowing which way to turn, I let you use me,
Waiting with open arms, you abused my love.
I loved you so well, would have done almost anything for you,
To prove this deep love I had inside me.
You still continued to play your mind games, derision ever present,
You watched my self-confidence fall into a decline, saying nothing.
For seven long years I cried for you, almost died for you,
                                        love of my life.
You never cared enough to understand how I felt,
Yet you told me years back, you loved me, I believed you,
                                        such was my mistake.
But sadly as I remember the blue of your eyes,
The truth has now proven itself over and over as I recall your many lies.

I am better now, there is life after you, but the time it has taken
                                                    to understand this,
Has taken its toll on me, both physically and emotionally,
Thank you.

Amanda-Lea Manning

INTRUSIVE REALITY

Reality is intrusive over the dream
Dreams are never what they seem,
Torn apart by a hateful circumstance
Loves lost and any future romance.

For the sake of future bliss,
I wave goodbye and the salty tears I kiss,
Reaching out I hug the air,
Life was never fair.

I'm engulfed in torturous tears,
I know he feels my pain and shares my fears,
He'll be in my heart and mind,
To have so much in common is hard to find.

Soulmates is a strong word but if time had been our friend,
We could have stayed together until the end,
Life makes a puppet out of our love,
But we need to keep our faith in the Lord above.

One day maybe in another life, we will meet again,
To beat the heartache and the pain,
Fate brought us together and destiny tore us apart,
I have to believe that some day we can be true to our hearts.

Kimberly Harries

YOU ASKED ME FOR A KEEPSAKE

When we were thrown together, we got along so well;
But you belonged to someone else, yet somehow I could tell
That there was just that certain spark our closeness could ignite,
And when we parted as good friends, I thought 'twould put things right.

We never knew the ecstasy to hold each other tight,
And no one knew the thrill I felt each time you came in sight;
They couldn't guess the pain I felt each time we were apart,
You asked me for a keepsake and I gave you my heart.

We knew that we were more than friends, with nothing really said,
We didn't talk of future plans, or think of days ahead.
But we decided wrong from right and vowed that we should part,
You asked me for a keepsake and I gave you my heart.

We both knew what was happening and knew it could not last;
I tried to keep things in control, but love moves much too fast.
I recognised the folly of our friendship from the start.
You asked me for a keepsake and I've given you my heart.

You asked me for a keepsake and I've given you my heart,
It isn't mine to do just what I want with anymore.
Though keepsakes seldom do get kept, please try to keep my heart,
Maybe the day will come and make it all worth waiting for.

Alf Godman

LOVE STRUCK AND HURTING

There he is, just seconds away,
But something tells me I shouldn't betray,
The pledge of fate that my heart is entwined by,
So, here I sit and cry and cry,
For my soul is longing to touch his heart,
And as soon as I've touched it, we'll never be apart,
So, forever here I sit, and cry and cry,
As, the clocks go ticking, and the clouds go rolling by,
And the day passes quietly on,
As a Protestant I sit, and hope the troubles are gone.

Should I approach her, the swan of the Belfast Lough?
For she is the beauty, that has provoked my every thought,
We sit just centimetres apart, yet, in real life we are separated
By a mountain of hate,
For our people know nothing but to fight and to bait,
So, here sits I, and cry and cry,
For my eyes are longing to see the ocean of thought deep inside her,
So, I will treasure this moment forever, and hope it will recur,
But yet what have I got to lose by talking to this jewel,
For she could never be, in my own eyes, cruel,
The day cannot go passing quietly on,
For as a Catholic, I will no longer sit, and wait
For the troubles to be gone.

Oh my goodness, the Gabriel of my heaven approaches,
He mustn't know that I cannot concur,
To those intense eyes and that witty tone.

My angel has rejected me, I feel so lost and so lonely,
She must think I'm ugly and I need a more toned body.

I love him more than life itself, if we were dead we could converse,
As a Protestant girl I live in hope, and wish that the troubles
Would end or *never get any worse!*

My angel rejected me, and the day rolls quietly on, and on
The lips of everyone in Northern Ireland is the word *fear*,
As a Catholic boy I live in hope, that one day
That *mountain will disappear!*

Danielle Elizabeth Thomas

LOVE BITES

Sudden intensity:
colours and lines.
Seeing, even in the dark,
your vivid eyes.

A fiercely pounding heart,
and ragged breath.
Is that how life begins,
after the little death?

The sweet moment passing,
your full lips blood-red;
your voice cool like crystal;
the harsh things you said

I knew love would kill me -
that was no surprise -
but why should the killer
have such laughing eyes?

Stephanie Cage

SUNDERED

Perhaps, in the old primeval flood
Some waves of our lives were fused,
But, darling, the flood is with us yet
To part us ere love is used:
Here is the dawn and here the night
In the passing moment of flux:
A moment to meet and know ourselves
And loving is the crux.
My poignant darling, how shall we rise
From this ever-thrusting tide?
Must we be always living and dying
To return to each other's side?

Pamela Constantine

FIRES

How you have lit
Such fires in me
Such scarlet flames
That dance and leap
And set my heart
And soul ablaze -
Then char and burn
And leave their ashes
Here inside of me.

What fire could ever burn away
The contours of your face
What flame erase you
From my soul
Could sear your gaze
Away from mine?

Small wick,
Sweet flickering candle flame!
A penny for your thoughts -
Scorched memories,
Charred time.

Carmel Wright

CORE OF THE FLAME

Hades is watching Persephone dance
The core of the flame blazing in his eyes.
The sight of her in that flowing blue dress
Makes him want to put down his pitchfork
And move to the Elysian Fields.
Why is it hell when you burn with passion?

He longs to declare his desire
But words keep getting in the way.
How can he keep her safe from the outside world
And hold her in his hands like a precious gem.
The lonely goddess of the harvest doesn't
Let him see her tears, as they turn into snow.

Vicky Stevens

LET ME EXPRESS!

Let me be free to express the feelings contained in my heart
by the chosen words spoken from my tongue
I see you - like one that would see a new rose
or the grace of a queen - you have ways that can be likened
to a slow-flowing river stream - offering a peace
as one walks its river banks - in return I sing your praise
that I believe could reach the Heaven's heights - and be among the stars
my love will remain with you until I am called away
by powers beyond my control - I will continue to value my days of life
still unknown to me and always share the feelings of my heart with you.

R P Scannell

NOT SAYING

Did I not say
I love you
Often enough
Did I not say
That so often
On seeing you
My heart did almost
Stop
I know now not
In those little gaps
Of I not saying
And you not seeing
So much was lost.

Geoff Simpson

DEAR BRIAN

He was strong in courage and in mind
With a will as strong as iron
To his children he was always kind
Dad, Grandfather, dear Brian
His shoulders, there for us to cry on
And generosity we could rely on
Now he has gone, our thoughts drift back in time
When dear Brian ruled over us sublime

Dear departed Brian, I often think of you
Especially on a Sunday, when I have nought to do
I wish that I had loved you more, but how was I to know
That God would take you from me and leave me sad and low
Eight years now I've missed you, cried at your photo's face
Especially when they play your song (and mine), Amazing Grace

Dorothy M Howell

A FLAME

There's a flame in my heart
And it's one you put there
It means we will never part
It means you always care

There's a burning inside
I love you more each day
There's a feeling that can't be denied
I love you more in every way

Long live our love
May it go on forever
Here on earth to heaven above
Long may it endeavour

You and I will always be
You who make me see

Philip Robertson

AUTUMN

The year is dying
and so is my love.

As he watches from his bed -
hips and haws turn blood-red,
and the leaves fluttering down
are scarlet, russet, gold and brown.

Weak sunshine slants upon
a pristine stately swan
as it glides towards the mill
on the river - darkly chill.

The day grows old,
as swirling mists enfold
meadows, hills and trees,
palely cloaked in mystery.

Dank earth reeks of decay,
a quiet stillness ends the day.
He turns his weary head to me
through blinding tears, I cannot see.

The year is dying
and so is my love.

Marjorie Beaven

LOVE IN ORBIT

You are a burning fire
of hope
you are the stalwart
of a forgotten race

You are the ensign
of humanity

To you I seek
for sweet embrace

You are my life
in another kingdom
you're my incarnate
my guiding star

You are my lover
my destiny leads me

To always be near
wherever you are

There is a mystery
sweet mystery in heaven

There is an infinite
we're infinite too

You are my lover
who calls when he needs me

Always - forever
I'll be there with you.

Mary Skelton

MY BEST FRIEND

Once upon a time I had a best friend
Strong in arm and of gentle heart
He meant the world to me
Amber eyes so bright and kind

Lips so soft and warm
He was loyal, brave and true
He fought long and hard against his ills
There was no more he could do

I lost him many years ago
This very good friend of mine
I never had a chance
To say a last goodbye

Many times I've wished to tell him
To stand by his side
To hear him say my name once more
Or touch his thick dark hair

We shared so many conversations
Even when I felt mute
He gave me strength and courage
He said I gave him hope

He gave me a poetry book
Called 'Our friendship does not depend on being together'
He was right about that, even in spirit John
You will always be my friend

Jeanette Jackson

THE FLAME

Let not the flame go out,
  The flame you lit in halcyon days gone by,
When life was but a dream and hopes were high.
  Now, in despair, you pose the question: 'Why?'
Let not the flame go out,
  Rekindle it with patient love,
And know, to give your heart and soul,
  To seek that one eternal goal
Is not to live in vain.
  Let not the flame grow dim.
Yet nurture it with all those memories sweet,
  Two lonely lives, that once were made complete.
Two hearts, that from their separate ways,
  Became as one, in better days
Than what beset you now.
  Yet know that death will have no part
In what you start, in years gone by.
  And questions, 'Why?' will hold no power to crucify.
So ask them not.
  Let not the flame go out!

A Roberts

ALL IS LOST

In silence I grieve,
That your heart could forget.
How should I greet you,
With silence and tears?
The sweetness of a flower!
I've lived in the misty solitude,
After the sad winds and winter's cold,
With many a thought of those dear,
And wished for years,
Sweet with summer's light.
Now, not a whisper, not a thought,
Not a kiss nor look of kindness.
I know all is lost.

Elisabeth Dill Perrin

MUSICIAN IN LOVE
(ON THE ROUTE HOME FROM HER DOOR)

He has soft airs on his lips; whistling quietly,
hearing tunes in every puddle-splash, crazy
rhythms in every uneven drip of guttering. The monotony
of the engine drone delights his memory
as he recalls the twinned heartbeat of their love-making. He is happy,
down to the hardened skin on the tips of his fingers, that are noisily
clicking and tapping beats on the wheel in a flurry
of sound that is edging towards the boundary
of what might be called melodic. But the drowsy
song of summer soon overrides his reluctantly
paused crescendo, as he slips up a gear smoothly,
aware of the wind flitting in and through the canopy
of trees as he drives further away
and, yet, somehow, nearer to her. The alchemy
she has bewitchingly and delightfully
cast over him makes him laugh out loud! Dreamily,
he plays the memories over in golden honey
colours in hid mind: coda, repeat, coda - they come thickly and brightly,
like the stars in a winter sky,
passionately refusing to lose their clarity.

Andrew Detheridge

MEMORIES OF LOVE

You were the love of night
that comforts in the silent dark of life.
You were the light of day
that breaks the dawn with tender touch.
You were the joy of life
the thoughts forever on my mind.
You were the winter and the summer of my life
since spring began.
You are gone.
You are the cold and lonely space.
The sadness of my life,
the memories.

Bruce Davies

TIME

Across the bridge of time, I hear you call my name.
Wait! Wait for me, you cry, and I shiver!
I feel your presence and hear the seagulls' mocking laughter
As they soar shining silver in the blue sky.

Love! Intangible! Untouchable! The wind and ocean hush,
As we reach across time to let our spirits touch,
Somewhere in time were we accursed,
And doomed to live apart, in penance for some crime.

Wait! Wait, you say,
So I turn from others,
Not knowing where or when
Or if we'll ever meet again.

Your voice and face invade my dreams,
Though we are far apart
And should we ever meet by chance
I'll know! By eyes, by voice and heart.

Then I will hold this precious time,
Hold it! in the palm of my hand,
Savour its sweetness like nectar or wine
For it may never come again.

Joan May Wills

ARTHUR

Arthur sat upon the throne, with Guinevere his queen,
Round table stories earned their place, his knights were ever keen.
He ruled a placed called Camelot, and a wizard he did keep,
A wise old man with spells and plot, would often haunt his sleep.

One fine day in England's spring, a lonely rider came,
Courage, loyalty, he did bring, Ivanhoe was his name.
He'd travelled far, to join this throng, and his devotion he did show,
This union they sealed with song, their future did not know.

This rare distinctive trio, in harmony did dwell,
Arthur's moods swung to and fro, his thoughts were hard to tell.
For many years, these knights were bold, their stories wrote a page,
Of history, that's often told, but glory turned to rage.

For on one lovely day in May, the spring festival began,
Guinevere with knight did stray, and into woodland ran.
This lovely queen, of faultless life, with Ivanhoe did roam,
And now she was a scarlet wife, her act, could not condone.

Arthur raged, then fell in tears, his lovely queen was gone,
His ancient order disappeared, his heart was full of scorn.
And into battle he did ride, his anger he would vent.
But victory herself did hide, his life was almost spent.

They carried him to Avalon, the hero's place to rest.
Here Arthur died, his legend safe, the ending of his quest.

Duchess Newman

WITHOUT YOU

Without the charms of your embrace
My life would pine away
With sorrow sculpted on my face
And dread of each new day.

Without the pleasure of desire
Each hour would be in vain,
Without your touch to light my fire
A chasm would remain.

Without your love I'd wear deep scars,
All wisdom would depart,
The sky at night would shine no stars
To light my broken heart.

Without you pointless days would drift
And flow lost on the tide,
I'd be a shell cast in the rift
Without you by my side.

You are my life, my world, my dream,
My mermaid found at sea,
You are the crest, the crown, the cream -
Without you there's no me.

Joy Saunders

QUEEN OF THE HILL

Hair like snow, eyes of blue
A heart that's tender, warm and true
We walk together every day
The sun shines bright, the birds are gay
Alas we are no longer young
But still we love the birds' sweet song
Perhaps as I look on the face
Of one so fair I find a trace
Of beauty that will last always
To cherish in my latter days
Am I alas too old to dream?
But on that fair hill it would seem
That age is many years away
She works her spell and has her way
And I am once more young and gay
Alas it is only a dream
I'll wake up soon and it will seem
We are a million miles apart
But still her face is in my heart

L E Growcott

LONELY

Long, long ago, to you I gave
Body, soul and all I had.
I have given much to save those
Around me that I love.

I was friendless - where were you?
Friends in those days were so few.
Many nights was I alone, forsaken,
Lonely and forlorn.

At night my mind is at its best,
I think about the love that left.
And that I reach out to the air,
I reach and cry, but you're not there.

I cry and wish that you were here;
To comfort me and banish fear;
To feel your arms would ease the pain,
And down my face hot tears rain.

In agony, I cry;
Dear God, I wish that I could die;
Where are you now? This feeling I hate
But I must bow my head to fate.

V Phillips

LOST LOVE

Unhappy day, oh! tearful hour.
A bitter cup, a perished flower.
My dearest love, doth fade away,
How can I meet the coming day?
How can my footsteps forward go?
How again can I beauty see?
My heart is full of bitterness,
Oh! why God should this fall on me?

Vera Porter

CUPID'S ANTICS

Cupid soars on clouds so high
And picks his victims one by one,
Then he lets his arrows fly
Till his mischief work is done.

The poor souls are thunderstruck
With a love that's unrequited,
Pale-faced, sad, and out of luck
They're not with lovemate united.

Lovers forlorn, in despair
Take to drink, to drugs or worse,
Sing sad songs upon the air
Self-destruct through Cupid's curse.

Why is love so mad, insane,
That it blocks the thinking mind?
The heart pumps, yet the poor brain
Makes the lover deaf and blind.

Each one wants what he can't get
Stays alone, or is mismatched,
It's most often a losing bet
Few love eggs have truly hatched.

I know well these Cupid tricks
And have scars that I can show,
Wounds that pride so painful licks
Don't ask me how come I know!

Emmanuel Petrakis

ADAM

Why do I think of him now,
When he is gone - left this earth

I just think of what could have been,
So close we seemed,
But it was for such a short time: - Why did he have to die

Why do I think of him now,
When he is gone - no longer to ail on this earth,

He was young when he went from this earth,
But still with treatment he kept his dignity

Why do I think of him now,
When his spirit is gone - his body no longer walking

Gone from this world,
From the place that treated him so shabbily,
So cruelly; with callous disregard,
They took his life, so jealous of his fighting spirit,
As he fought illness, cantankerous against sickness

Why do I think of him now,
When he is gone
When we never had time for the love we shared
Lassitude,
Languor settles in,
As he battles on for life,
He achieved a change of character,
His life shorn from him

Why do I think of him now,
Remembering him,
He is gone

Alison Carr

PRE-RAPHAELITE TRILOGY

Lizzie Siddal to Gabriel Rossetti - Feb 1862
Addicted to the poppy and to you I died,
and when coldly coffined felt a notebook
placed by warm and guilty hands
among the tresses of my once lauded hair.
Oh faithless one! Do you think your tardy words
will comfort in the silence of the grave?
Go, and let me rest in peace, for there is
nothing left for you to say - or me to do.

Gabriel Rossetti to Lizzie Siddal - 1868
My passions they are all aflame for brooding,
black-haired, swan-necked, Jane, and poems to her
I must disguise among those penned
to your bright eyes. So I'll disturb you one last time,
retrieve the notebook rightly mine, even though it's holed
right through by worms that must have bored you too.
Then I will publish, stake a claim to literary and artistic fame.

Lizzie Siddal's exhumation and revenge - Oct 1869
When the night breeze fanned my still bright hair, I sought his face,
he was not there. The coward from his task did shirk,
let others do his dirty work. But if he thinks he's done with me
he's wrong. I will not let him be. For taking what was rightly mine
I'll haunt him to the end of time. I'll see he dies by his own hand,
and joins me in this underland.

For him there'll be no RIP.

Doreen Dean

PATHETIQUE

Helen would stand
with her hand on the glass
and in her pensive mood,
leave as a dark cormorant
and skim the waves to Duart point
and back.

Heart below high water mark,
chained to drown
on the passing of an unseen moon,
her essence free yet captive
on The Maiden Isle,
the body stood
within ten feet of me
yet I could not, would not
break that reverie.

Washing through our minds,
(her's unaware of mine,)
each movement would unfold
a magic, tragic tapestry
of late lit waves in fjords
and all things unrequited.

Then, by the fourth,
I watched her breast
and saw we two were synchronised:
breath and treasured tears
measured by the music.
The siren's wax was melted from our ears.

John Tirebuck

THE TEARS ARE ALWAYS IN MY EYES

The tears are always in my eyes
Whenever I think of you
You're never far from my daily thoughts
No matter what I do
I think of all our happy times
The laughter and the fun
The holidays we used to have
And lazing in the sun
But you left without a single word
And I never heard again
And all my lovely memories
Were overshadowed by pain.

The years rolled on, I married
But never forgot you
I tried to get on with my life
What else could I do
But you were never out of my thoughts
So the tears still came to my eyes
Oh why did you have to leave me
Without ever saying goodbye
I could have handled it better
If only I'd known why.

J Gilchrist

Sometimes

Sometimes situations get out of hand
say wrong things, misunderstand
life turns out nothing like we planned,
sometimes we regret the things we say
and in the end there is no way
the debt for us to then repay
you have to know I still love you.

Sometimes it's hard to then forget
things that caused so much upset
now a lifetime of regret,
sometimes I know I should have tried
to close the gap that grew so wide
but I thought that time was on my side
you have to know I still love you.

Sometimes I look at what went wrong
to turn the clock back how I long
realise at times I stood too strong,
sometimes I think it's easier to pretend
that broken hearts can never mend
and it's safer to defend
you have to know that I still love you.

Sometimes I feel the need to write
to try and end this pointless fight
and to the darkness bring some light,
sometimes I feel that I'm to blame
somehow deserve the guilt and shame
and though it could never be the same
. . . you have to know I still love you.

Paul Langley-Punter

A CHANGE IN THE WEATHER

For days late summer heat had built
Hazing first fields of corduroy
Where swallows climbed the heavy air
To shimmer over distant wheat.

Dense storm clouds mass as black night turns
And thunder stumbles round the hills
Until a brief fluorescent flash
Illuminates our airless room.

Then rain. First heavy drops explode
Unevenly in ones and twos,
Till suddenly a torrent grows -
Setting awash the window sill,
Racing down gullies, blocking drains,
Cascading from gutters, swamping
Lawns . . . everywhere is overfilled.
Later we hear the storm's last roll
As timpani begins to slow:
Rain shushes to a steady drip.

And under blankets of warm air
We lie and wait for ragged dawn -
Together, but with separate thoughts -
Aware, like love, that summer's gone.

P B Osada

LOVING THOUGHTS

Will I ever forget you my love . . . your special presence?
For in you was me . . . and what affected you . . . affected me.
You being there made me into what I am.
I am just now . . . as I am . . . as best I can . . . but without you.
I sometimes wonder who and what I am?

Margaret Kaye

IN A DREAMWORLD

An Italian sonnet for the one I crave
See how she goes without me
The clouds are grey all around me
Ready to pour on my grave
Reaching to be saved
By a love that's not to be
But the truth I refuse to see
In a dreamworld I'm totally enslaved

Drifting away on a gondolier
On a water that's so cold
Not as dark as what's in here
The pain that fills my soul
Away from me she disappears
Her night journeying forever rolls

Rodger Moir

UNDYING LOVE

I met him before in a past life,
oh yes, I do know him, there's an affinity, a belonging
I feel a sad longing, we stared, this was the one and only
but I felt an awful fear of dread within
yet I know I cannot be without him,
he came, there was no word spoken, we just embraced -
with kindred fire of love we knew our fate
another lifetime gone, another chance is here
once again a war, he did not return, another lifetime
I lived with a lonely heart deep, deep within
never ever to forget. Here I wait till my river of life ends
but when will true love meet again on earth
I sense the presence of his loving soul
waiting, longing with undying love and I fear not death,
it is sweet, hurry that we may be together forever.

A B Lawson

A TASTE OF LOVE

When I was young I met a girl,
Who threw my head into a whirl.
She made me wish to skip and dance,
So one day I knelt and took a chance.

She looked, she laughed, she said, 'You're kidding,'
'Oh no, when you're close, my heart starts skidding.
Out my body, across the street,
Then helplessly beats, by your feet.'

She said, 'You fool, you can't love I,
For soon my love I'm sure to die.
For cancer holds my final end,
So just be close and be a friend.'

'Oh love me please, until you go,
And then your love my heart will know.'
The love she gave, she taught me well,
And now my heart, of love can tell.

For we were just two kids at school,
She the princess, and I was the fool.
Six weeks, no more, and she was dead,
But love we shared is in my head.

Eleven years that maid was here,
And as I age, she still feels near.
She taught me death cares not for age,
And I must live till my last page.

Sid 'De' Knees

DESDEMONA AND OTHELLO

Desdemona, a beautiful creature
was set up by an unknown feature
so happy and so in love
her and Othello were like two doves

Then one sadden day
after Othello came back from being away
she stood accused of having an affair
that was something she would never dare

The pain that soon filled her heart
was like an arrow pierced it with its dart
as she soon dies to Othello's sword
with her soul departing to the Lord

Othello now all remorseful for his sin
lay still looking at the tin
the tin that formed part of the sword
sees him also depart to his beloved to the same accord

Kristina Howells

DON'T TELL ME

So much was done and
Much more to bear
Thou have gone away,
And wilt thou crown
My beshevelled name?

But who cut the bond?
Do not pass away . . . nay,
My spirit lingers,
From when love suffered,
Without thee, where art?

Ah, but few could dare,
Palm to lips,
I am not serene,
'Til thou return,
And bravely suffered so.

Yes, glorious eve,
My endurance weeps,
There is no grave
And 'twas no birth,
Repose is my woe.

To have an unchained soul,
I prithec an image,
Of thine sweet dreams,
While thou have gone,
'Don't tell me'.

Linda Curtis

LOVE'S EMBRACE

I fear I've fallen from your grace.
I no longer feel love's embrace.
I miss your kiss,
And your touch,
As much . . .
Your hand
Upon my hand,
So passionate,
So full of hate.

Clare Todd

LONG ROAD

My love is like a shining star and will always shine for you,
The light may flicker once or twice but will always remain true.
Attraction may not be as strong but caring is still there,
And whatever comes our way I'm sure we can share.

When once we were so positive but now we have our doubts,
Life is one long road to travel and changes vast amounts.
But the journey has nearly ended and we may have reached our goal,
So now let's tread the path of truth and reap what we have sown.

We must now think of being positive and set the wrongs to right,
Whatever's gone before us we must truly put from sight.
Each one of us is different and we may not stay the same,
But let's look to the future and not from whence we came.

Irene Morgans

ROMEO/JULIET

Our love was conceived
in silence, darkness.
Listen, I did not lie
your hand on my heart.

We spoke no words
nothing to say, sighs
finished. Fire dying
your hand touching mine.

Day too, broke gently
before blackbird called
I remember final moment
when I turned and kissed you.

T Webster

EVENING SONG

I'll take you down to the country and lay your head to rest,
besides the flowing river beneath the maggies' nest.

'Oh God why have you taken her?'
My life is stripped of zest.
I feel no love for man nor beast,
On her vision, I no longer feast.

When will the pain begin to wain
When will my memories fade
Forty years of endless love engulfs
My heart and mind.

Goodbye my virgin, mother and friend
You're mine for evermore
Listen out for my gentle knock
On Heaven's cottage door.

David Bilsborrow

COUSIN SELINA

For her they wished a dazzling life
with sunlit skies and a white house
and horses. And a yacht swinging
at anchor against a breakwater -

none of the struggles they had had
when they were young. As man and wife
they put their backs into her life,
counting every pound and penny.

So he was wrong, John Highlandman,
from when they got together, failing
the grade, out of sync, far from
the one to be her one and only.

The summer swims, they didn't matter,
the afternoons on bikes, the swirl
and spin of giddy quickstep nights,
nor moonlight on the winter river.

She was meant for gaudier fish
trawling on a grander ocean,
with gorgeous fins and bank accounts
calculated to enchant her.

All this put paid to him, of course
and to her, the loving daughter.
Now the sun behind the pier
and shining roofs, lingering,

and never again his foot on the stair
to start the rib-eye steak and candle-
glow and that fool clarinet
making midnight on the radio.

Josephine Brogan

OUR TIME

I see you staring back at me,
Happy and content,
Sharing our lives together,

But your eyes have closed.

I feel the warmth of your smile,
The way it lights up your face
And shows the warmth within you,

But you are now so cold.

I remember the good times,
The sharing of thoughts and ideals,
The embraces which enveloped us,

But these are all I now have.

I know you will be waiting to meet me
When it is time for us to be together again,
I wish every day to be reunited with you,

But I know it isn't my time yet.

Lindsey Hood

GENTLY

Gently he laid down beside her
touching the crest of the wave
her body so beautiful
a statue carved with pride.

Her eyes shone like a million stars
his passion hot on her lips
her body moved . . .

now was the time to say yes.

Alison Hitch

UNTITLED

Your love is dead.
My eyes devoid of your laughter.
My cheeks white from desolation.
I do not know where you are
I know not what you do
In times of harsh winds,
I think of you.
The smell of our flower, musty with age
Wipes away the now.

In love I let you go.
In solitude I yearn for your touch
Oh how I wish you were near
Close by.
I am lost and you are too far away to know.

Emma Bingham

SECRET DREAMS

We laugh and talk about my secret dreams,
Joke about my wild romantic schemes,
Just you wait, I say, the day will come
When I shall find the perfect man for me.

He may be tall and handsome, short and fat maybe,
But when I look into his eyes
I'll know he's the man for me.

We'll walk thro' fields of clover,
Paddle in the sea, hold each other's hands
For the whole wide world to see.

Wander down the leafy lanes, 'neath the starry skies
Love's light glowing in our hearts,
And shining in our eyes.

He'll hold me in a warm embrace
Whisper tenderly,
Slowly turn around, and walk away from me.

Wendy Dawson

HAIKU AT STREAM BRIDGE

I stand on this bridge
looking at summer's beauty
dancing in the breeze.

Each flower reminds me
of that laughter in your eyes
and your slenderness.

As the leaves caress,
buds suckle the morning dew -
eager as your lips

once sought my embrace
throughout our summer's summer
blessed with happiness.

Tall hollyhocks wave
where the honeysuckle scent
excites desire -

stirs those memories,
those hours of perfumed passion
gathered in moonlight.

The murmuring stream
like your breath which cooled my brow,
whispers messages.

I reach for your love
but it drifts like these waters -
beyond life's garden.

R H M Vere

HER SILENCE

I can do nothing with the moon;
It drifts, irrelevant, with stars.
The troubadours forsake their tune
And soon abandon their guitars.
Why should hope wither and decay?
    You do not say.
    You do not say.

Your silence, like a shroud, descends
Upon our scarcely-born desire,
Ensures its infant life now ends
And our bond fail. Why did our fire
Not burn beyond its tinder glow?
    I do not know.
    I do not know.

Norman Buller

A GIRL'S LAMENT

He said that he loved me and I was the one.
I was his earth, his moon and his sun.
So I believed him, it felt so good.
I was his Marion and he was my Robin Hood.

Always together, our life was wild.
But here I am caring, for our only child.
This is the story, no happy end.
He is now round the town, romancing my best friend.

He was my first love, maybe my last.
Who wants a woman, with a family and a past.
Why was I so stupid, so taken in?
A victim in this world of physical sin.

My parents don't want me, there is no one there.
If I cannot manage, my child will be taken into care.
I cry my heart out when I'm in bed.
When I think of all the pillow talk that we said.

I loved him dearly, this was my fate.
I did not know how love can turn into hate.

E Napper

You Don't Need Me Now

No, my friend you don't need me now
It's funny how things have changed
We don't stay, the way we were
Maybe it's time to say goodbye.

Just stop and think
I thought we were friends
I guess, that was only me
Your work is your life
I am no further use to you.

I am sorry; it had to end this way
My thoughts will be with you
Please take care my friend
May our Lord look after you.

When you stop to think
Maybe, one day you will see
Footsteps in the past
That will be me
I promise, I will walk softly.

Have a good life.

Carole A Cleverdon

TEARS OF DESPAIR

Tears fall gently from my eyes,
Run down cheeks, onto pillow fly,
Self-pity, thank God there's no one here,
To see my pain, this awful fear,
Why cry for others' hurt and pain,
Emotion - there is nothing to gain,
Still the tears fall, will not abate,
Why me - get in this awful state?
I cry for all this hate-filled world,
For man's misdeeds that have unfurled,
I weep to feel my mother's touch,
Now gone, I miss her oh so much,
The words of love that were not said,
Now an empty world - filled with dread,
Please - sweet release - my tears still flow,
Despair at feeling at such a low.

W Curran

HANDPRINT

Archaeologists find a handprint, a rose in stone beside
The bones of a couple in love.
Our spirits say leave them be, but the lab beckons.
Separate on a shelf of skulls after 200 years.
I will find you again, we will go to heaven.
Paris a golden age, the handsome cabs and stage.
Writers write and artists paint.
The Moulin Rouge, the Eiffel Tower, where does the time go?
When is to dream a loveline and show?
'When love is timeless', William Shakespeare once said.
Take a riverboat down the Seine then you will know, scientists bah!
With chemicals of analysis recreate a face for all to see.
Never recreate our feelings for one another.
This they could never rediscover.
The moon so tranquil over Venice, such beauty graces my eyes.
Take a gondola to a masquerade ball, in life the dancing fireflies.
A bloom to my darling, we dance until morning.
How sweet an aroma, how sweet the rose.
Our love will be eternal like the cosmos.

Barry Powell

SONNET TO ROBERT

Love came late, by fate deferred, but coming
Relit the brave, bright flame of youth anew,
Setting my quivering heartstrings humming
A hymn of joy on golden wings to you.
Love came late but, came at last and living
Unravelled its true reason and its rhyme,
Gloried in the selfless act of giving,
Beyond all earthly space, beyond all time.
Love came late with wisdom, truth and seeing
A heart so empty, desolate, forlorn,
Revealed to the essence of my being
Its very aim and purpose to be born.
I love you truly now as I did then,
For all of distant time beyond our ken.

Joan Weston

A LONG GOODBYE

The more I open my heart,
The tighter you smother my dreams.
The longer I show my love,
The stronger you turn away.
The deeper I hide my emotions,
The more of me I lose.
Stifled and suffocated into obscurity,
Leaving little options -
- no other redress to choose!

Gary J Finlay

DAWNING

Amidst the seemingly endless sleep in timeless zone preceding dawn,
When widows' wives and willows weep and gale invades
                                        the sinuous town,
And counterpane is little shield 'gainst storming elemental rage,
The sweated brow and fisted hand lash meekly at imagined fiend.
And twisted body wild with strain cavorts in anxious disarray.
But time the healer of all wounds becalms the slumbered agony.
And come the morning's welcoming light, fly to the arms of one
                                        who cares.

Baydon N Greenway

JUST A SMALL MIRACLE

Not too much of a miracle
Just a little one would do
Enough to help me cope with things
That are making my life blue
As the future opens before me
Let at least a glimmer of light
Appear to assuage the darkness
And ease the Stygian night
I know I can never forget him
I know he will always be there
But leave my pride with something
Do not let him see how I care
If I should see him tomorrow
Let me go out in style
No weeping as I say farewell
Please at least let me manage a smile

Barbara Williams

LOVE IN DESPAIR

I'm suspended between two worlds,
Full of hurt and pain.
Filled with love, I can't let go of,
Hoping we can meet again.

The happy past, the hope of future,
The nothingness between.
I can't go back, I can't go forward,
Wanting us to be again.

Are you so perfect? You judge me so harshly,
Throw me away again.
Leaving me with love I can't let go of,
Full of hurt and pain.

P Merrill

LIKE A SHIPWRECK ON A DESERTED BEACH

Like a shipwreck on a deserted beach
Our love lies forgotten
By the cruel world of people
Who resented our love.
Who begrudged us our happiness.
Ours was sublime love
All consuming,
Full of uncontrollable passion.
A living thing
Thriving on the fulfilment
Of a dream,
Shared by two naïve souls;
But crushed and broken
By prejudice and ignorance,
The shattered pieces brushed aside
Destined to lie
Like a shipwreck on a deserted beach.

M S Reid

IDLE CHATTER

You thought that idle chatter was enough,
If we don't disagree we must get on.
But what about the questions left unasked about
The thoughts still deep inside, you'll never know?

You know more of me than many other people,
But you are satisfied with what I choose to show,
You have never really tried to understand me
Or asked me how much more there is to know.

Janet Fowkes

WAITING

We fell in love quite late in life,
We felt it was meant from the start,
You longed for me to be your wife,
I loved you with all my heart.

We had to wait for many years,
For long spells away from each other,
Your voice on the phone was music to my ears,
You were *always* sure *one* day we'd be together.

At last we were rejoined my love,
As we knew we were meant to be,
So happy, contented and at *last* your wife,
Every moment spent so happily.

We knew our love would always remain,
And then you were ill and taken from me,
But I'll always be proud to bear your name,
Till together once more we will be.

D Carne

YEARNING!

My heart yearns for a lover,
She is so near, yet far,
My love for her shines brighter
Than any heavenly star!
Alas, she loves another,
And every time we meet,
A fragment of my broken heart
Lies shattered at her feet!

A E Garrod

DROWNING

You leave me -
drowning
in this
sea of dust -
so I curl up
beneath the waves
and dream of
mermaids -
called Ingrid.

Ken Price

PLATONIC

Like penfriends, they were companionably sweet,
He floated like a spirit, so they seldom met,
Then he'd fill the gaps with words, vivacious words,
And was full of life when they did meet,
Breathless with news of trees, plants, rural charms,
Apprehensive, too, about the town's filth and harms.

His talk was studded with literary gems,
Hardy, Proust, Joyce, even Verlaine,
Who'd have thought that Branwell B would loom
So large, or that kidney-eater, Leopold Bloom.

For months he would completely disappear,
Then, shining, on the scene, he'd reappear.
A card from France, resurrecting again
Kings, queens, princes, their battles;
A card from dark, troubled Moscow,
She'd hear his footsteps on the snow.

An airmail from Tangiers rattling with bottles:
Rummy tales, she'd smell the wine.
A dispatch from crowded Argentine
Gay with song, ringing with vitality.

Then, unexpectedly, from New York, a card
Yearning for his own backyard,
Lonely for his own small backyard.

She liked that missive best of all.

Mary Frances Mooney

FOOLS AND BROKEN HEARTS

Fools and broken hearts go hand in glove
Well, here I go again, falling in love
Falling for you again, what can I do?
There's no one else for me, it's always you

You want me, you need me, that feels good inside
Then leave me, that grieves me, and tears at my pride
For you know I'll be waiting here on my own
You know I'll still be here when you get back home

I'd give all I have if I could just find
The key with the answer to the ways of your mind
Then I'd know why you love me, then leave me this way
And know why I'm sitting alone here today

I'm a fool in love but what can I do?
There's no living for me, when I don't have you
I know you'll return and I wait for the day
Yet know in my heart, somehow, you'll never stay!

Karl Jakobsen

THE STORY BEGAN LIKE THIS . . .

He waltzed into my life
With a charming smile,
I thought he'd be mine forever
But he only stayed a while.

He stole my heart
And left, never to return,
He took me in, threw me out
Leaving my life in an emotional whirl.

He was so close to my heart
The person I loved most of all,
I trusted him completely
With him I could stand tall.

In the time that we shared
I learnt so much from him,
He'd been hurt in the past
Unknowingly he ended up hurting me.

Now every night before I sleep
I pray to God up above,
That God presents him with most precious gift
The gift of love.

Rina Begum

WHO'S THE LOSER?

We were very close, remember?
You loved my every move
I saw you as my real life super-hero
You saw yourself as my owner
I would do everything you told me to
You would always have your own way
I never argued, I feared your fists
That's why you would always win
Is that really to be proud of?
I'm trying to move on now
I've got my life on the right track
But in the end you'll be the real loser
'Cause you'll lose me.

Stacey Tully

IF ONLY

I tried so hard to be with you
Hold you close and say goodbye
But all I can do is hold your hand
And ask God 'Why did you have to die?'

What will I do without you
Throughout the coming years
Will I be able to think of you
And not shed bitter tears.

How will I tell our loved ones
You have gently slipped away
Will we find strength without you
To get through every day.

Half of me has gone now
We have never been far apart
But I still have happy memories
Deep within my heart.

Every day we said, 'I love you'
But now it's time for me to go
With a heavy heart I will kiss you
And whisper gently, 'I love you so.'

Pauline Drew

MARGARET

We were two innocent sixteen year olds
With nothing but love in our hearts,
And we never imagined the day would come,
When our lives would be torn apart.

She was a beautiful dark-haired girl
With a smile that came from the stars,
Hers was a wealthy background,
While mine was well below par.

Her father was a very rich surgeon,
Who had often wished that she was a son,
To go into the field of medicine,
To succeed him when he had passed on.

My dad worked in the bowels of the earth,
An over-worked underpaid miner.
Who struggled to bring up a big family,
But no man ever proved finer.

Apart from our social divisions,
Religion came on the scene,
For mine was firmly entrenched in Rome,
While her spiritual head was the Queen.

Her father firmly explained to us both,
That chalk and cheese will not mix,
And he barred us from seeing each other,
By adding a threatening prefix.

That if the liaison continued
His parental thoughts would become nil,
And he would disown my Margaret forever,
By cutting her out of his will.

Then fate took a hand in this story,
Before Margaret was seventeen,
She became seriously ill with Polio,
And her soul departed from the scene.

A postscript I must add to my story,
To prove how bitter men can behave,
For I was banned from the funeral,
And warned never to visit her grave.

But material things will all vanish,
And social divisions will end,
When we meet again in the future,
And above hatred our love will transcend.

Gerry Concah

BEYOND THE PANE

I never look up into the star-filled night
As we did then.
Two faces turned towards the glittering light
Under a winter moon.

I never can find the group of stars
You said was mine.

But if through rain-washed windows
I see the stars are there beyond the pane,
I do look up and search the sky
And say your name.

Kate Davis

SUBMISSIONS INVITED
SOMETHING FOR EVERYONE

POETRY NOW 2001 - Any subject,
any style, any time.

WOMENSWORDS 2001 - Strictly women,
have your say the female way!

STRONGWORDS 2001 - Warning!
Age restriction, must be between 16-24,
opinionated and have strong views.
(Not for the faint-hearted)

All poems no longer than 30 lines.
Always welcome! No fee!
Cash Prizes to be won!

Mark your envelope (eg *Poetry Now) 2001*
Send to:
Forward Press Ltd
Remus House, Coltsfoot Drive,
Peterborough, PE2 9JX

OVER £10,000 POETRY PRIZES
TO BE WON!

Judging will take place in October 2001